Dreams

Randy B. Ephraim

ISBN 978-93-5610-150-0

Published in India 2022 by Pencil

Contributors:
Editor: Becky Jenkins

A brand of
One Point Six Technologies Pvt. Ltd.
123, Building J2, Shram Seva Premises,
Wadala Truck Terminal, Wadala (E)
Mumbai 400037, Maharashtra, INDIA
E connect@thepencilapp.com
W www.thepencilapp.com

Author biography

Randy Ephraim was born in Port Harcourt in 1991 to a family of three, he happens to be the last born with two sisters.

He studied Engineering in the Rivers State University. He has written several stories unpublished.

He wrote his first published story in 2013 for a Comic Company in college called Genefex.

Over the years he went into music and songwriting he has written stories for small groups and theaters.

He started writing poem in 2007 and ever since has written over 100 poems used in events and adverts.

He's a teacher and music lover.

CONTENTS

Dreams.......... 8

I have a dream.......... 11

My heart inside this note.......... 13

I am yours.......... 16

Love Story.......... 18

Drunk in love.......... 19

Little miss sunshine.......... 22

heart Ache.......... 24

- Burnt.......... 25
- How did an angel break my heart.......... 28
- Brilliant Mystery.......... 30
- The pain that wont go away.......... 31
- Ink reveals the mind.......... 32
- My Africa.......... 33
- My new Italian Shoe.......... 34
- Sound of victory.......... 36
- Act of the mind.......... 37

ANOTHER TALE.......... 39

- My dream, my fear.......... 40
- Truth in Lies.......... 43
- Identity.......... 45

Introduction

'Dreams' is a collection of some favorite poems, short stories and quotes of the writer, stemming from his long delusional ideas, midnight fantasy and fictions, to his complex love relationships.

The writer tries to tell a story about himself highlighting through his poem's personal experiences in phrases like clues of his footprint of events and situations he has been in, both depicting his down moments of love and despair, his long obsession of a glorified idea with images drafted in perfection and subjected to false scrutiny. His ideas about life are quite prolific, such open mind, like a man lost in the jungle (unfamiliar terrain), but then his Jungle is his world surrounded by family of which he felt lost, lost in the midst of his crowd, struggling for years to find himself and most times search for satisfaction in things and people.

Demoralizing are these circumstances especially in an individualistic world where everyone seems to be concerned about themselves more than others, on the path of his search he was often faced with disappointments, often time he was left on the mountain top alone, consumed with fear he felt he was going to fall.

Moments when his thoughts became his omen.

Haunted by the same image he created; his ideas became his omen.

Over time he creatively built his castle and concept on beauty and nature, most of which are till today his inspiration. His absurd way of expressing displeasure was born from his early age when he constantly suppressed his anger, rather than speaking out, he clamours silently at every oppression and drowns away his pain in a world created in his imagination.

Dreams is indeed a private collection and tells mostly of the writer's personal life tales and stories.

These dreams are his beauty spoken in poetry.

Dreams

Woke up to the grinding sound of a carbonated generator set staring the cool morning vibe into a terrific war-fare. Just at The Silence of my dark room littered with unwashed clothes and unread books adorned with my new sheets not quite a week old, I turned stretching my arms towards the left close to my bed stool Heaped with engineering documents, just underneath it was an electric extension socket connected with wires, one of which curled like a snake to the end of my bed bonding passionately to a white case which often times over-served its use as it is programmed with a Ringer for morning calls and deep night illusion stories (my mobile phone) when it breaks in with a ring from someone who needs to hear my voice, not always pleasant though as we were belied years ago of spirits calling at night to steal your soul.

Falsity clouded our minds, hopes ran out of fear as men put upon themselves shield of resilience.

The old age was one-of-a-kind mostly seems to have means of solutions when they draw big lines on sickle babies to change their reincarnated looks trying to stop them from dying, if it be by any means the pains of the children giving back their strength, fear of them from further brutality or God being loving to the children, somehow, they tend to recover.

I grabbed my white case still fevered by the un-deteriorating noise to check the time of such intrusion to personal comfort, it's 40minutes past the 5th hour of the day on a Saturday, just then I had a feel-good hormone running through my heart down, weekends are not so much of a terror like the day after tomorrow offers.

In just a split second my mind threw up, carving its dented mark on my cheek pushing the two sides of my lips upward like a curve reducing gradually my eyes…

someone else seems to be giving me delight.

Just a year ago I was alone with no love from a woman, but the thought of her calmed my mind. From her last message, I perceive love seemed not so far anymore.

I probably have one of the most boring love stories never told. Ironically, there was never a love story, just heartfelt emotions twisted in uncertainty, it's nothing extra ordinary; probably the wrong orientation or just on the thought of dreams come true but the fear of it breaking foundation is another.

Just turning to realize that there has always been a fear just like in the old age, funny enough nothing has changed only improved from one form to another, who knows this might just be a new theory.

These few months have been the most threatening of my life as my future tends to be standing with a dagger on a battlefield, the fight of the future rumble but no one is fighting, just me and my fictitious ideas which seems to be leading nowhere, for me I'm

dedicated and aiming for the trophy of victory without sentiments…

for once I'm willing to let go.

It will be hard to draw a line in my existence and tag as fear of Relationship as it may seem, because the proclaimed fear is tied to sincerity, to be in that ideal and perfect relationship such as my eyes only saw from a distance with a small wall built over it…

I believe this fight will lead to several things,

And mine is just starting.

My lineage has just begun… Its more than just a dream

I have a dream

I have a dream
The world is yet to see
My dream, my hope,
More than a fantasy

My thought runs deep.
My plans not cheap.
I fear letting it out,
Only finds comfort in my heart.

But night came and sun rose,
Dreams where gone, change arose.
Eyes grew dim, heart grew weak.
Puzzle changed; dreams misplaced.

Hopes tumbled
Fight for the future rumbled
No light to brighten my path
No thought, no muse, no sight.

But right at the silent darkness I will arise
With a heart burning with passion
Right at the finish line will I raise the flag
Victory is won at last.

I have a dream
The world is yet to see
My dream, my hope,
More than a fantasy

My heart inside this note

My heart inside this note
If it were one of my vibes, I would have added a quote
Unfortunately, anger, betrayal and frustration as my heart wrote
So, I'll pour cold water so they all can float.

The agony of failure has made me to cry
I lost my love because I was shy
I noticed I couldn't do somethings, always scared to try
Now she's gone to another and her letters I can't reply.

I know if I were a man for one hour, she would have stayed,
and the mess she's in won't have been made.
If I had just a little gut, she would have been saved
then this sad note won't have been written.

I write with tear drops falling on my sheet
My love left me when I didn't even cheat
Maybe it takes less than faithfulness to

cause a breakup.

Maybe not being man enough can cause a breakdown.

She's exposed to the world and it's all my fault

She might lose her pride which will bring her hurt

In the traps of false tales from friends she's caught

I let her go not knowing when I did, my actions spoke louder than words.

I was wrong in different ways

What she wanted was in my diary back in the days

I desired to please her, though her thoughts weren't plain to me

The reason for me being shy is my love and desire to maintain her wish.

All I was trying to do, was to make her what she wants

giving her a smile and taking all the hurts

All I wanted was for her to be mine

Now she's gone and I'm sad and she's fine.

I've never loved before

Didn't believe I was in one until I was told,

I pray it isn't

I wouldn't want to experience my first in this way.

I miss you
You won't realize it
I love you
Please how can I emphasize it.

The beauty I can't explain
Whose love to me sustains you in vain
Whatever I have I will give to you
Don't even know why I keep running back to you.

I can get my mind off you, but I choose not to
You're better than those I'll want to put my mind on trying to stick to
I need an angel to make you give me the chance
A chance to put your heart back in my hands.

I am yours

He:

If humans are purpose ,

Then I'm fulfilled.

While men struggle to discover,

I knew mine with just a smile.

A smile that poured hot ice to my vein.

And comfort to my mind

Just a thought of you

Feels like heaven.

Men in past have died for love;

Just to prove their love

But with you, it's new.

Death has no place

He knows how crazily I want to be around you.

If you wave at me,

I wouldn't ask for more than a smile.

If you smile at me,
I wouldn't ask for more than you staying a little longer.
If you stay a little longer,
I'll only let you look into my eyes.

To see how much of you have been built in me,
To see how your smiles have enslaved me
To know how your absence crucifies me
And how much your presence energizes me.

When you're not there, only you are the substitute,
Please have all of me without gratitude.

Love Story

My eyes fell to the ground
As hers humbled me
I delayed, stood for a while
Just to gain courage,
All of this reminding me.

My foot dashed the ground at my last experience,
And one even prettier is before my presence
I thought the minute I lose my breath is the day I die,
But for half an hour my body stood fixed,
Only shinning eyes gazing at the mystery of my world.

My heart raised a secret alarm.
The greatest thing only common to angels have struck my arm.
This must be a charm.

My eyes have met my dreams
My love psalm.

Drunk in love

If I write my confession
It will be painted with tear drops
And lines from the side of my palm
Imprinted on my sheet.

If I'm to say my possession
Rating them in naira or thrones
They'll break into ashes
And fall like rain.

If I try to sing my thought
My chord will hold down the longest note
Till it chokes me up
And I'm left with no tone.

Swallowed in my thought…

If my memories are something
Then I'm hunted by the same image I created

My worries being nothing more but karma
Then no doubt I'm being paid more

But who am I to measure the destiny of two?
When my heart awaits trials to be divided in two
Left with broken pieces to fix
Tears and blood being piece

confession…
This is a license to diss.
Words no longer hurt.
My love came so strong.
Left on the air with no place to fall.

I gave up my heart,
Tied my hopes to the flames,
This seems to be my story
Whenever I choose to be real.

I'm sorry it came in like this,
What can a man give when left with nothing but tears.
Perhaps these words will be tagged in my diary,
Hopes smashed when drunk in love.

I can take out my heart for you and hope not to die.

I'll take the world for you if that would be the price.
My love is true and I'm glued,
Because I can't live my life without you.

I can say you're beautiful
But you wouldn't understand
Your gentle heart kills me with each word you say
Let me catch my breath because I'm overwhelmed
Now I'm crying out loud because you still won't understand.

your smile is short yet makes me laugh,
I want you more in each passing time
A girl like you is too hard to find
I'll give my all for another chance

I'll be a clown to make you laugh
Get my hands burnt to make you lunch
Fight a thousand with the last drop of my blood
Tear my heart in two so you'll see it's been
sold to you till it gets old.

I thought I knew defeat
Till I thought of losing you.
Scared of the words you'll say when I tell you
I love you.

Little miss sunshine

Dark clouds can't take away your beauty
Its glow changes in hidden places.
Fairies are the most beautiful story character
But you're the most beautiful story maker,
I know many fairies who will die to be like you.

Funny I call you sunshine
Where the sun at night is displaced;
You're not, always shinning
I thought of buying you a diamond ring
But its radiance cannot outshine yours.

Let me take a walk with you
Kingdoms can fall, rainbows can crawl
They won't create as much attention as you.
You're like a case study with no reference
Like the stars of the heavens for multitude
You need no light to be at the spot

Beautiful things don't look for attention
They just can't be hidden
I almost lost a breath when I first saw you
Now I'm not scared of losing it if it's just to
be with you.

heart Ache

Burnt

I loved you
Even when you hurt me,
I loved you.
Cause love never turns nor goes away.

It's a choice we make
And I choose to love you.
And in the wrong choices I've made
The greatest is you

I'm not ashamed to say I was wrong
I'm glad I did
The joy and laughter you gave me
Is unexplainable indeed.

It's like a miracle before my face.
My sorrow met with grace
The different dagger you stabbed me with
Just pumped out my heart more for you.

I never knew I would be so comfortable
with pain and tears and still stick with you
I could still trace that little smile from
the side of my cheek
As tears roll down my face.

my dilemma…

I'm fed up, trying to write out my hurt
That I've given up on this long complex progression
Even at this point of my writing
I still feel like falling.

Enslaved to the torture of your love.
When it ties and chokes me
I still struggle for air just to think of you.
Do I say I'm obsessed with you?

I'm so weak and tired
My eyes have cried out so hard
That it's lost in space of awkwardness
Time has eluded my awareness.

I'm vexed by you
You were gone even before I could say goodbye to you.

The wound in my heart will always remind
me of the lovely pains I shared with you.
And the terrible fact that I'll always love you…

How did an angel break my heart

I stood and gazed in front of her
Knowing she knew all I would be
The perfect love I carry
For her, the part that blends with me.

She never said those words
Yet I poured out my all
With the charms in her eyes
Propped my heart in different styles.

Sometimes love never turns around
You'll see me melting in her arms
A world of endless pleasure
A world that surpasses all treasure.

Together our hearts denote
I'll be gone for long not knowing my return
said her note
My soul and perfect mate
Left before the date.

My eyes brought out blood
My heart gushed out mud
Goodbyes were not expected in our path
How did an angel break my heart?

Brilliant Mystery

Sizzling things in beautifully ceased chords
Tumbling thoughts from rumbling words
Schematic on display in this solid disdain
I'm pricked and numb, it feels like I'm in sane.

Is it from my so desired love affair?
Or my reality in whose colors I share
Dashes of blue, gray and black in shades
Painting its colors on my skin like lines marked with blades.

It's the joyful sound of a feminine voice
The longing dream of myself design poise
Fudged in a holistic dose of ache
Publicly caves me and keeps me awake.

My voice engraved in the heart of my choice
My smile unveiled in the voice of my love
This brilliant mystery is the coat of my life,
And I must marry it as my wife.

The pain that wont go away

Scratching my inner soul,
It's itchy, so I scratched further
Peeling out the outer surface.
But then the itch went deeper.

Like a scavenger I tore every piece.
Ate off my fingers and ignored every diss.
Like a cannibal I broke my bones
Dug into my flesh to pick out the bones.

I ran to the edge of the room to find a minute rest.
Shielded by the shadow of a faint light,
I struggled for air as the silence ceased.
My bane has been released.

My fingers were painted with blood.
my soul and misery have created a bond.
My silent clamour could not free me.
I was born with this fear; you cannot save me.

Ink reveals the mind

Pen void of words
Mouth dried of ink
Gushing out emptiness
From its hallowed blank vacuum.

Writing its letters home
No words only cracks to show its storms
As it wallowed in space
Filled with faint dark light.

Thought sparks in time
But mostly overcome by the dark
Its power fades in space
Sniffing for that faint dark light.

But in that hallowed blank vacuum
are encrypted signs that says;
"The ink refills the dried,
The pen reveals the mind."

My Africa

Africa my Africa
Glory of the nation
Breast of motherhood
In our long quest for victory.

Let the world hear her heart and come
From the beat of the Ogele to the wobbling sound
The heavy breath of great men
As their heart's strokes to the steps of destiny.

Great Africa,
Beauty in diversity
Great Africa
Compliments the world in totality.

My new Italian Shoe

Empty with a narrow heart
Covers her pain, carving on a muddy path
Transcends sometimes, glamour's at spot light.
Faintly upright, yet shows great might.

Her love at the prince's heart
Staring up desires, looking intact
Despite her size and chemically pasted mat
She captivates the eyes with great delight.

Lowly laid back to the ground.
Smoothly laid heart to the sand
Held with a precious hand
She's conspicuous more than diamond.

She's pleasant to behold
Never grows old or gets cold
Never sad on soft and tough mood
She sparks at dark cloud, highly valued to be sold.

She's narratively expressed

Overtly impressive and never oppressed

Adorns the road to fame

Her beauty gladdens my heart.

She is what men use to walk miles

But with her empty narrowed heart she carried me with a smile

Oh! truly she is my new Italian shoe with black

and brown zebra style.

Sound of victory

Raging sound of a joyful song
Strong sentries defeated young
A tribal cliché with one voice
Clicks a victorious chaos.

A long-lost song arose
The exodus of her clan raises smiles
Earth, ugly and dead
Sand, dread and weird.

Charisma lost in drama
Royalty stumbles to a farmer
Grasses forcefully pricks its garment
Red river flows with raging sunset.

Joy lost in joy
Cloud smiles at earths bark
Bare in large covering of one
Sounding cuckoos like a trailers horn.

Act of the mind

Need ways to calm my nerves
My anger is kindled, my feet losing stands
About to decide with no form of romance
Though not given to taking decisions by chance.

My anger fueled my pain
Burning with thoughts of revenge
My hard work feels in vain
Consumed and drenched.

Dump them in pay back
Leave them with nothing to lay back
Teach a lesson of control
This I lament as anger clouded my soul.

I've aligned their faults, and vexed by their flaws
Discipline them with all strength in my bone I thought,
But these faces are people I love
While others; problems I need to solve.

A disciplined leader I am.
One with love and grace, a good heart.
Though these acts of revenge have clouded my mind
They are just thoughts in my head.

ANOTHER TALE

My dream, my fear

It all started on the 1st night.

We gathered round a dim light.

We muttered loud our thoughts in cheese of whose opinion was circular.

While I dashed away pons and checked the Queen in Particular.

It was a night in quote.

My heart in court sworn to an oath

The who I thought she could be

The one whose thought clouds my fantasy.

Like glass I mirrored my thought

In terrace to my breaking point.

I sussed her stacked moral preamble

She's like gold yet so unprotected in her circle.

I made the first move

Like Chapman I imagined a Smoove

Walked to her with words of pretense

Not denoting the desire in my sentence.

I started with “hi” so you’re” Lola”
That means you’re from Yoruba
Writing a Song lyric is giving me wahala,
Please can you help me with a native
song in Hausa?

She thus consented to help
Smiles popped because I just crossed the first step,
We continued our conversation online
Tried to know her more and make her mine.

Days slept on by
Questions left all why
We slowly left our distance
Together we were the next instance.

We spent time together
Each day beats the other
She’s hospitable and superlative
Like oxygen, I felt I needed her to Live.

I’ve dreamt of committing to a girl
One that is satisfying and beautiful as well
Never understood How it will feel
Didn’t know when in owe of her I fell.

She's more than I imagined
She's more than imagery
Like the silent sound that echoes at night
It frightens me yet comforts me.

It's crazy how I'm still jailed to her
Even when she's not a jailer
I find myself climbing to her
Though she's not a skyscraper.

She's like an adventure
And I don't have to travel miles to get to her.
She's like an addiction
I'm obsessed with her.

The way she diss me
It shows she misses me
The way she holds me
Just shows how much she needs me.

What I wanted was to know her
And possibly love her
Now all that scares me
Is falling in love with her.

Truth in Lies

In this note this tale of her I tell
Journey through the crossroads
Hiking down deep Valley
Drowned in illusions, painted with uncertainty.

The track of my race has been erased
Left with memories as hallow as the dimples on her face
She was all that filled my mind
In those brief moments our lies we shared.

Our fractions merged like we are meant for each other
We lived in deceit, now we are believers of this order
Our bond strong in this brotherhood
Mated from the ovaries to the fallopian tube.

We shared our joy in those rare moments
It Blooms increasingly each time we spent.
Every fascinating moment together,
being deluged in reverie of each other.

I really like her I lie not.

Belie my feelings in the state of it being completely sold out.

You my dear have proven to be a perfect flirt.

So skilled and guile, can make a nomad stay.

Driven by your complexity I became a fan.

Glued to your live show of deceitful affection.

In this delusion I'm caged and Quarantined.

Lost in your lies, it feels like a whole new horizon

Your rare rage and poise are artistic.

Like a brilliant mystery behind a painting of an artist left to be unraveled.

You my lady are my muse.

In this truth in lies and infused.

Identity

Me, myself and I
Standing all alone,
Beaten by the rain, cold to my bone,
Is it the life I've lived or the seeds I've sown?
Are there others like me, or these thoughts
are just my own.

I've been soaked in the fumes of choices I've confused.
Told a lie, ruined relationships, true friendship
I've abused.
Broken promises and resources I've misused
Then I ask myself: WHO AM?

Am I the family to which I belong?
Or the many melodies in my song.
Am I that reincarnated son's soul super-imposed
in my body?
Or the outcome of the play mummy and daddy
had the other morning.
Am I the result of the broken promises of my father?

Or the ill words spoken by his mother.

Because when I do wrong, they'll say you're so stupid

I guess that's why I've not been shot with love

arrow from cupid.

Wait! Wait!! Wait!!!

I perceive it's from my childhood

I heard my stubbornness precedes me because i grew up in the hood

Exposed to abuse, yeah mummy and daddy were not home sometimes,

Times when I silently screamed my hurt,

Still trying to hide the scar lines.

When the night seems far from morning

And I had to go to school late

When my breakfast comes hours past morning

And I project far to see the meal in other people's plate.

I was drained of love, only found comfort

in my phone

Looking up dirty sites, exposed early to porn.

Drowned in my quest for sex, tried so hard

but could not stop.

I asked myself in all of this, do I hold someone

responsible or it's all my fault.

Yet again I ask myself WHO AM I?

Am I the job I do?

Or the money I make

Am I the value of my suit,

The car I drive or the cake I bake?

In this confused state I ask myself, WHO AM I?

Those moments when I feel fear feeds false

festival of defeat

And victory is on a long race.

When joy escapes and envy employ devious

destructive devices deeply void of dignity

And life seemed like a wild chase.

I ask myself, WHO AM I?

I'll picture this and FRAME IT on the wall

I am not what you've seen through the picture of time

I'm not the option of my once deluded and wrongly influenced mind.

I am the light of the world

A city on a hill that shineth more than halogen bulb

I am the offspring of righteousness

Signed, sealed and sanctified, birthed in godliness

Broken and bruised I seize to exist

Yet in another life form my life is preserved, and

this is not another gist.

Some have been lied to

That to their problems there's no end
That on this road they're on is curled in
addiction they'll have to bend.
That life is worth the seeds in past you've sown
On the road to redemption there are no
crowns nor thrones,
But these are just lies tied to your defeat
Cause Christ death on the cross redeemed
you and buried your past in the pit.

Therefore, I am John 1:12 who received
power of sonship
Like him who died in Colossians 3:3
and his life could not fit into an A3.
His grace has made me stable
So, I can say No MORE TOSSING
I mean NO MORE TO SIN
Cause sin is not in my nature,
Sin is just another picture
Sin is just a state
Sin is not my mate
It has no power of me.
On these truths I stand
I am the direct reflection of Christ
Lost to his Lordship and driven by his will
I am not ordinary, I am not normal.